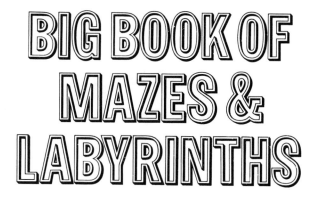

BIG BOOK OF MAZES & LABYRINTHS

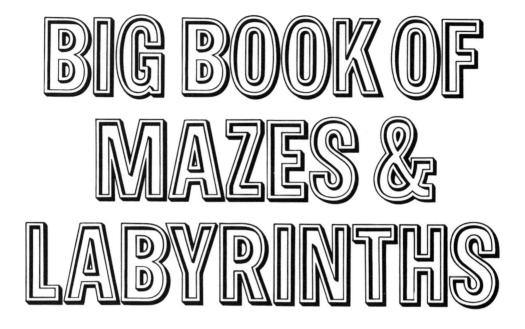

BIG BOOK OF MAZES & LABYRINTHS

WALTER SHEPHERD

DOVER PUBLICATIONS, INC., NEW YORK

Published in Canada by General Publishing
Company, Ltd., 30 Lesmill Road, Don Mills,
Toronto, Ontario.
Published in the United Kingdom by Constable
and Company, Ltd.

Big Book of Mazes and Labyrinths is a new
work, first published by Dover Publications, Inc.
in 1973.

International Standard Book Number: 0-486-22951-3
Library of Congress Catalog Card Number: 72-97817

Manufactured in the United States of America
Dover Publications, Inc.
180 Varick Street
New York, N.Y. 10014

CONTENTS

MORE AMAZEMENT vii

THE MAZE PROBLEMS 1
  1. A Lunch Date 2
  2. A Flight of Fancy 4
  3. The Man in the Moon 6
  4. A Mayday Frolic 8
  5. Weathercock-a-doodle-Do! 10
  6. Bad Karl's Cavern 12
  7. A Game for Easter 14
  8. Guy Fawkes Night 16
  9. Collecting Your Baggage 18
10. Start the Day Clean! 20
11. Ringing the Changes 22
12. Color Bars 24
13. The Four Seasons 26
14. The Soccer Game 28
15. A Christmas Tree 30
16. A Proverb in Practice 32
17. Percy's Problem 34
18. Unlucky May 36
19. Underground Movement 38
20. New Year's Eve 40
21. Hit the Coconut! 42
22. Home on Leave 44
23. The Magic Barometer 46
24. Willie the Worm 48
25. Roll Out the Barrel! 50
26. Talking Turkey 52
27. 'Twixt Cup and Lip 54
28. A Spy Hunt 56
29. Waste Not, Want Not! 58
30. The Chunnel 60
31. Postman's Knock 62
32. Here's Luck! 64

33. The Giant Firecracker 66

34. Coil and Recoil 68

35. Welcome Home! 70

36. The Village Postman 72

37. A Shunting Problem 74

38. Going Camping 76

39. The Old Nichol 78

40. Fire! Fire! 80

41. The March Hare 82

42. A Christmas Cracker 84

43. Adjusting the Time 86

44. Getting Away with It 88

45. The Four Winds 90

46. The Surplus Domino 92

47. Put Your Foot in It! 94

48. Your Shot! 96

49. Jumping the Queue 98

50. Man on Mars 100

HOW TO SOLVE A MAZE 103

SOLUTIONS 105

MORE AMAZEMENT

The first series of these puzzles (*Mazes and Labyrinths,* Dover, 1961) contained a brief account of the history of mazes and labyrinths. It was there told how the ancient idea of the labyrinth as a prison without doors, from which escape was nevertheless almost impossible, was adopted and adapted by the medieval Church to provide a compact path for pilgrims to follow on hands and knees by way of penance. Such paths were set out as patterns in the colored tiles of a church floor, often at the west end of the nave.

Fig. 1. The octagonal maze at St. Quentin, measuring 42 feet in diameter. A similar maze in Amiens Cathedral, dated 1288, was destroyed in 1708.

The general plan of these mazes is nearly always the same, and they consist of a single, forced path to the center, with no choice of ways. An example is shown in Fig. 1, and the sixteenth-century Italian maze in Fig. 2 is but a slight variation of it.

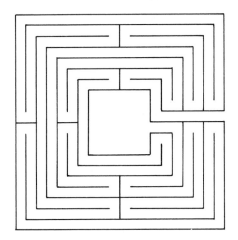

Fig. 2. A plan for a maze published in 1537 in an Italian book on architecture.

In England, the old mazes seem to have been used more for amusement than exercises in piety, for they are not found in the churches but in the open air. Their paths are usually marked out as ditches cut in the turf of a hilltop, or enclosed between low turf walls. In gardens, the paths are often separated by trimmed hedges, and these may have sprung from the garden topiary work favored by the Romans.

Fig. 3. A Dutch design for a garden maze. (After H. E. Dudeney.)

Mazes of this kind were in evidence in some medieval Italian gardens, whose "geometrical" or "set" designs became the fashion in France, Holland and England in the sixteenth century. A Dutch garden maze with a forced path is illustrated in Fig. 3, while Fig. 4 shows a proposed plan for a garden maze published in 1706 by the designers of the famous Hampton Court maze.

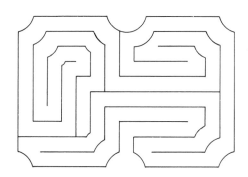

Fig. 4. A proposed plan for a garden maze published in 1706 by the designers of the Hampton Court maze.

The open-air mazes were often very much larger than could be laid on the floor of a building, that at Saffron Walden, for example, measuring 110 feet in diameter and covering about three-quarters of an acre. Threading the mile-long path of such a maze could be a wearisome experience, and the dizzy finisher of the course might well exclaim with Shakespeare's Gonzalo:

> By'r la'kin, I can go no further, sir;
> My old bones ache: here's a maze trod, indeed,
> Through forth-rights, and meanders! by your patience,
> I needs must rest me.
>   —*The Tempest*, iii, 3.

The Saffron Walden maze consists of a forced path of the ecclesiastical type, but the idea of devising a puzzling network of paths with choices of ways to confound the hasty seems to have antedated the introduction of the classical labyrinth from the Continent. In Iron Age times the entrance to a fortified settlement was often a maze of passages carefully planned to confuse an invader, and to force him to expose first his left side and then his right to a hail of stones and arrows from the barbicans.

The largest and best known example is that called Maiden Castle, in Dorsetshire, which was developed about 250 B.C. from a Neolithic and Bronze Age hill-camp already 3,000 years old. It attained its greatest elaboration in the first century B.C., but was finally conquered by the Romans.

Situated on a flat hilltop 432 feet high, it was about 1,000 yards long and half as wide, covering some 45 acres. It was surrounded by a series of enormous ramparts built of chalk, soil, clay and limestone masonry, which towered 50 feet above the narrow passageways between them and increased the total area of the settlement to 115 acres.

There were maze-like entrances at both the east and west ends, but the north and south sides were protected by continuous high ramparts three-fifths of a mile long. In Fig. 5 these have been drastically cut so as to bring the two maze entrances together and show their combined plan. As a problem, this looks absurdly easy when seen from above, but it was quite otherwise to an invading army marching in single file between steep walls as high as a five-story house. It was impossible to see far in any direction, or to guess which way to turn at each corner. The wrong defile might lead to an ambush or a surprise attack from the rear, and if an entrance to the fort was finally found, the cunning provision of a hidden second entrance nearby enabled an immediate counterattack to be launched on the flank.

Well, it was a sort of three-dimensional maze, owing its effectiveness to the height of its walls, but it was intended to bewilder and not merely to exhaust, and so is basically different from the Cretan Labyrinth of tradition. The original Labyrinth at Cnossos was probably not a maze at all, but merely the intricate jumble of rooms and corridors which formed the enormous Palace of Minos. See Fig. 6. The very word "Labyrinth" is derived from the non-Greek word *labrys,* meaning the double axe, a common symbol on the walls at Cnossos, which could hardly have been planned to confuse the residents!

Fig. 6. Part of the ground-floor plan of the Palace of Minos, at Cnossos, as unearthed by Sir Arthur Evans during the first quarter of the present century.

Visitors to the palace, and perhaps prisoners attempting to escape the dungeons through the vast ramifications of the sewers, may often have been unable to find a way out, and so a story got about which later became the famous legend. There was certainly a "Mistress of the Labyrinth," and the Minotaur which inhabited it was evidently a particularly cruel king who may have thrown his prisoners to the bulls, to be tossed about before the girl toreadors gave their performance. But the idea that the Labyrinth was a purposely constructed puzzle-building arose only after several centuries of oral tradition.

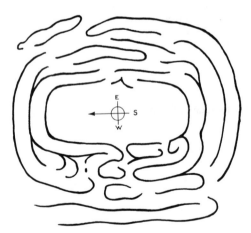

Fig. 5. The east and west entrances to Maiden Castle, brought together by shortening the ramparts on the north and south sides.

On the other hand, the Middle English word *mazen* always meant to puzzle, bewilder or perplex, and the oldest reference to a maze in English, in Chaucer's *Ariadne* (*c.* 1385), compares the classical Labyrinth with the familiar English maze:

> . . . the hous is krynkeled to & fro,
>   And hath so queynte weyis for to go
> For it is shapen as the mase is wrought—

Another legendary maze now believed to have been merely a large rambling building containing many rooms and corridors is that known as Rosamund's Bower. Here, at Woodstock (in Oxfordshire), Henry II is said to have kept his mistress safe from the jealousy of his wife. That was 800 years ago, but though some ruins in Woodstock Park were being shown to visitors in the seventeenth century as the remains of this maze, it is more likely that Rosamund was kept in a house perhaps comparable with the Market Cross House at Alfriston (Sussex).

This is an old Tudor inn (still functioning) whose numerous rooms, both upstairs and down, contain an enormous number of doors. Unguided visitors soon lose themselves, turning up repeatedly on the same landings, or reentering rooms they have already vacated several times. This inn was once the haunt of smugglers, and its maze of doors provided an easy way of dodging the "Preventive Men" (coastguards).

As long ago as the first century A.D., Pliny described the ruins of an ancient maze at Lemnos which probably also belongs to this class. It is said to have contained 150 columns "so perfectly balanced that a child could turn them," and though it is not certain what this means it suggests a hall with 150 revolving doors—surely a dodger's paradise!

The method of eluding pursuit by dodging through doors or round corners was practiced by the inhabitants of a criminal ghetto in the East End of London about a hundred years ago. Known as the "Old Nichol," it was immortalized by Arthur Morrison in *A Child of the Jago* (1896, but often reprinted). In the novel the district is called the "Old Jago," possibly to commemorate the Reverend Osborne Jay, the local vicar who worked among the "Jago rats" and eventually got "the blackest pit in London" demolished and the entire area reconstructed (1900).

The Old Nichol consisted of 20 narrow streets containing 730 terraced houses, in which nearly 6,000 people lived, and the police never ventured within its boundaries except in numbers. The houses had no frontdoors, these having all been used for firewood, but presented rows of rectangular black holes into any of which a fugitive might dash. Since the houses or their backyards were all connected in one way or another, he might reappear at almost any other black hole in any neighboring street, and immediately vanish again.

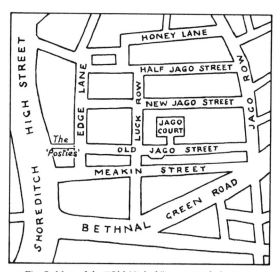

Fig. 7. Map of the "Old Nichol," a criminal ghetto in the East End of London a hundred years ago, described in 1896 by novelist Arthur Morrison as the "Old Jago." Morrison's fictitious street names have been given and the map has been slightly corrected. The "Posties" was a narrow foot passage barred to vehicles by posts across one end.

Fig. 7 is a plan of the Old Nichol showing Morrison's fictitious street names, most of which are parodies of the originals. It is a fair example from real life of a type of maze sometimes used in our puzzles. The map in puzzle No. 39 includes the district as it is today, Old Nichol Street being Morrison's "Old Jago Street," Boundary Street his "Edge Lane," Brick Lane "Jago Row," and Redchurch Street "Meakin Street." ("Honey Lane" ran from the bottom end of Virginia Road.)

For some centuries there was another London "maze" in the borough of Southwark, at the south end of London Bridge. Here, the walks and gardens of an inn called the *Abbot of Battle,* together with the alleys on the other side of the street (now Tooley Street), formed an area known as the Manor of the Maze from before 1386, and it was still being called "The Maze" in Victorian times. It is commemorated today by such names as Abbot's Lane, Battle Bridge Lane, and Maze Pond (now a short road).

The latest maze to appear in London is the decorative symbol on the new Victoria Line platforms of the Warren Street underground railway station. Warren Street was probably named after Admiral Sir Peter Warren's daughter, who married the first Lord Southampton in the seventeenth century, and the maze symbol, illustrated in Fig. 8, is a pun on her maiden name. It is, perhaps, intended to amuse people waiting for their trains, and it presents choices of ways at several points.

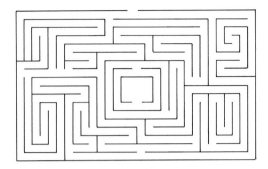

Fig. 8. The maze design used as a symbol on the platforms of Warren Street underground railway station, on London's new Victoria Line.

However, mazes with single forced paths are also constructed for amusement, and we have illustrated two in Figs. 3 and 4. To thread such a maze, walking toe-to-heel, has always been as popular with the very young as—let us say—walking along the top of a wall, and Oliver Goldsmith remarked in *The Traveler* that:

> Dames of ancient days
> Have led their children through the mirthful maze.

But it cannot be denied that such mazes have also fascinated older people, and some have considered the labyrinth with a forced path as a fitting symbol of predestination, the maze puzzle presenting choices of ways standing for the principle of free will. These moral aspects of the maze have been appreciated from the earliest times, so we are not surprised to find in John Harmar's translation of Beza's* sermons, dated 1587, that "Salomon . . . hath walked vs through the whole labyrinth & mizmaze of this life." And Milton himself uses the same image of those who:

> . . . reason'd high
> Of Providence, Foreknowledge, Will, and Fate—
> Fix'd fate, free-will, foreknowledge absolute—
> And found no end, in wandering mazes lost.
> —*Paradise Lost,* ii, 558–61.

So the story of mazes and labyrinths, like all good stories, has its moral—somewhat obscure, perhaps, but by no means to be omitted. And after that—why, the puzzles, guaranteed for amazement only and free of all moral implication!

(For a mathematical approach to the solution of mazes, there is a section at the end of the book on "How to Solve a Maze.")

---

*Théodore de Bèze, 1519-1605, a French-Swiss Calvinist reformer.

THE MAZE PROBLEMS

No. 1
A Lunch Date

Having arranged to disclose some secret information to Sergesuit Spykovsky over lunch at the Wonder Bar Grill, double-agent Shady Brace had difficulty in finding the right table. Spykovsky was sitting at the top (right) table for two, but Brace actually visited all the other tables before finding him. In doing this he sometimes had to retrace his path between the tables but he never needed to cross his own tracks. What was his most likely route?

Note: *To "visit" a table means to touch the SINGLE line edge of the tabletop. You must follow an open path between tables, being unable to pass where the way is blocked by chairs, tables or people.*

No. 2
A Flight of Fancy

Visit the harem of your dreams on the magic carpet! Start at the bottom (center), and if you can get across the carpet to the top without making more than three mistakes—well, we wish you an enjoyable weekend at the harem!

Note: *Dreams are said to last only a few seconds. Allow yourself no more than 30 for this one!*

No. 3
The Man in the Moon

The Man in the Moon, laughing heartily at some of the headgear worn by Earthlings, decided to interview one of the four characters shown here. Cadging a lift on a returning *Apollo,* he managed to track his chosen specimen down. How did he go?

Note: *Select one of the four figures first, and then find the path from the center to that particular one. (All four may be visited.)*

No. 4
A Mayday Frolic

The yokels (A, B, C) have got the three ribbons of their maypole (numbered at the top) a bit tangled. See if you can trace *by eye alone* who holds which ribbon. If you have a stopwatch, time yourself and your friends to see who has the quickest accurate powers of observation.

Note: *This is a "solid" maze, the ribbons running in three dimensions and being represented in perspective. So where you can see that one ribbon runs behind another you just go round with it, and if the ribbon is twisted—well, you don't bother about that, either.*

No. 5
Weathercock-
a-doodle-Do!

News comes from all quarters. Start at the "N" and spell out the word "N E W S" without crossing a line or using the same path twice.

Note: *How many other words can you make out of the letters N, E, W, S, using 4, 3 or 2 letters?*

No. 6
Bad Karl's Cavern

Karl's bad—there's no question of it, for he once trapped Patrolman Footsore, tied him up and threw him into the set of caves now called Carlsbad Caverns to commemorate the incident. Patrolman Footsore eventually got free of his bonds and set himself to find a way out, being careful to leave notches on the wall as he went so that he should never cross or retrace his path.

It so happens that in escaping he went through nearly all the 38 "doorways" between the caves, yet he never passed through the same one twice. Had he gone through *all* the doorways he could not have escaped at all. What is the largest number of doorways he could have passed through, just once each, and yet still escaped?

Note: *"Doorways" means, of course, the narrow gaps between the caves. The puzzle may be solved by trial and error, or by a simple mathematical inspection.*

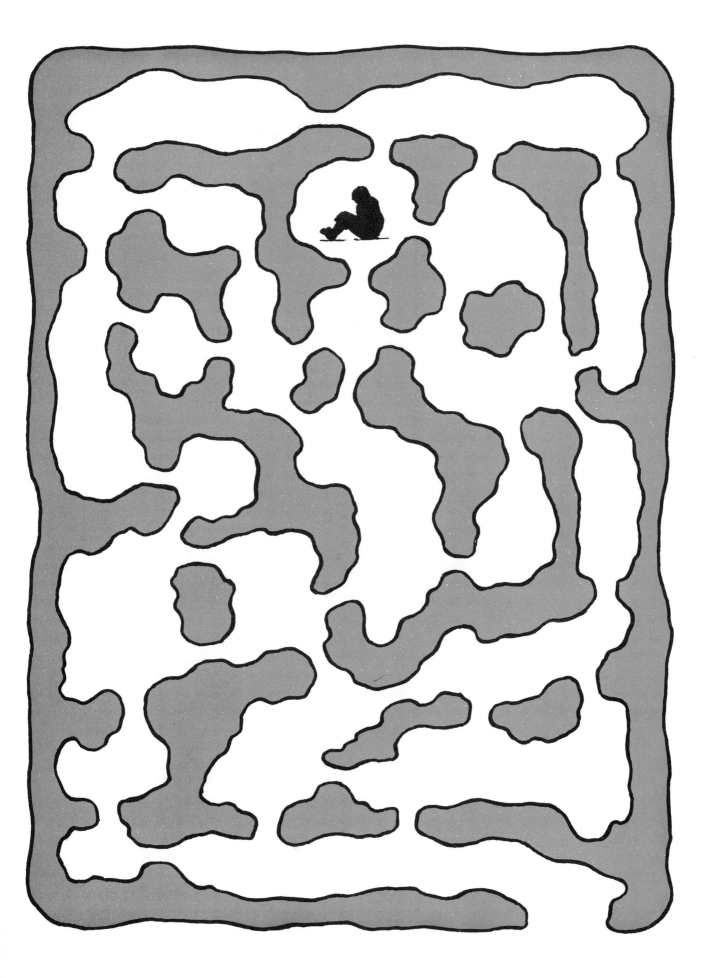

No. 7
A Game for Easter

You take one shot each, in turns, and each player is allowed three shots altogether. Starting at the arrow, you must aim for a different prize each time, so that if you win them all you get the maximum score of 35 points. You must follow each turn through to its end, and may never retrace your path. If you arrive twice at the same prize you may take a compensatory 3 points for your second visit. But if you arrive by mistake at the soda-mints, your whole score (up to that point) is canceled.

Note: *To play solo, declare in advance which prize you intend to get, and then see if you can win it first go.*

No. 8
Guy Fawkes Night

As an excuse for letting off fireworks the British still burn effigies of Guido Fawkes, who tried to blow up the Houses of Parliament on 5 November, 1605. Well, see if you can light all five firecrackers, and the bonfire, *with the same match!* You may not use the same paths twice, nor cross your tracks—and, of course, you must choose the right match to start with. Which is it?

Note: *Before the day, children parade their home-made effigies round the streets, crying "Penny for the Guy!" to collect money to buy fireworks.*

No. 9
Collecting Your Baggage

You ask for your baggage and the cloakroom attendant says, "Help yourself!" So, starting at the arrow (bottom), collect the three numbered bags in order and return with them to the counter. You must collect the bags by their handles and may not use the same path or path-junction twice.

Note: *The three bags should all be collected on the one journey.*

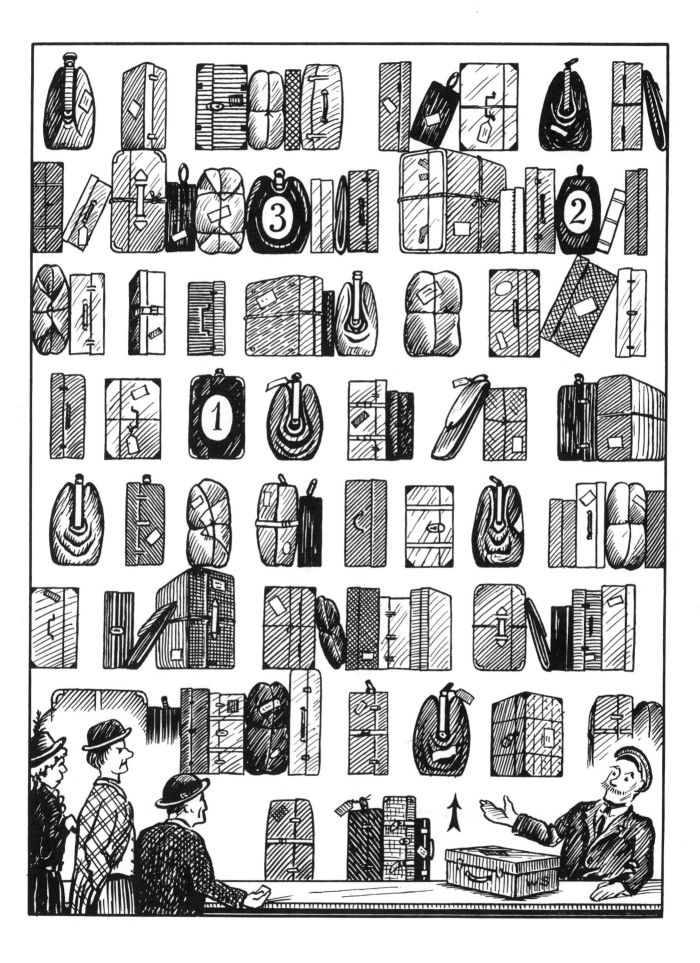

No. 10
Start the Day Clean!

Soapy Sam was an old soak—but not the sort you mean. He loved to start the day clean with a nice hot bath, but always managed to lose the soap for so long that the water got cold. So he invented the floating soap cake shown here. This had a bubble inside so that it floated on top of the water, but it was hardly an improvement because it *would* swim away to the foot of the bath where Sam couldn't reach it without excruciating pains behind his knees. However, you may manage to get it for him without any pains at all, starting from the nail of the pointing finger, but you may not cross any of the lines.

Note: *There really are—or have been—soaps that float like this one, so don't rush off to the Patent Office!*

No. 11
Ringing the Changes

In what different orders could you pull these four ropes (A, B, C, D) to ring the "BELL" at the top of the page? You must trace the ropes to their right bells *by eye alone,* but you may let one rope stay idle, if you like, using the same rope for the two "L's."

Note: *This is a "solid" maze, and when one path runs behind another you follow it around regardless of the lines crossing it.*

No. 12
Color Bars

These country inns are all named after colored animals (if we count man). Starting at the Blue Boar (bottom, left), make your way to the Pink Pig (top, right), passing all the other six inns on the way. There is only one way you can go without using the same roads twice. Which is it? Give the answer as the order in which the inns must be visited.

Note: *The bars are all open if you feel thirsty!*

No. 13
The Four Seasons

Start at the SPRING (top, left), and run through the seasons in order (SUMMER, AUTUMN and round to WINTER), without crossing or retracing your path.

Note: *There is one other traditional season—the "silly season." When is it supposed to be, and why?*

No. 14
The Soccer Game

This is a pinball machine on which you play a kind of soccer. Choose a side and see if you can score before your opponent. Center Forward (C.F.) kicks off, and then play continues from black to white and vice versa alternately, but always along the lines marked out. You may not return the ball along the line it has just arrived on, and when it is your turn you must take it before your opponent can say (clearly!): "Soccer—soccer—soccer—soccer!" (four times). If you haven't moved by then he can take your turn for you and follow it with his own.

Note: *The other initials stand for Goal Keeper, Left Back, Right Back, Center Half, Inside Right, Outside Left and so on. Not that it makes any difference what you call them!*

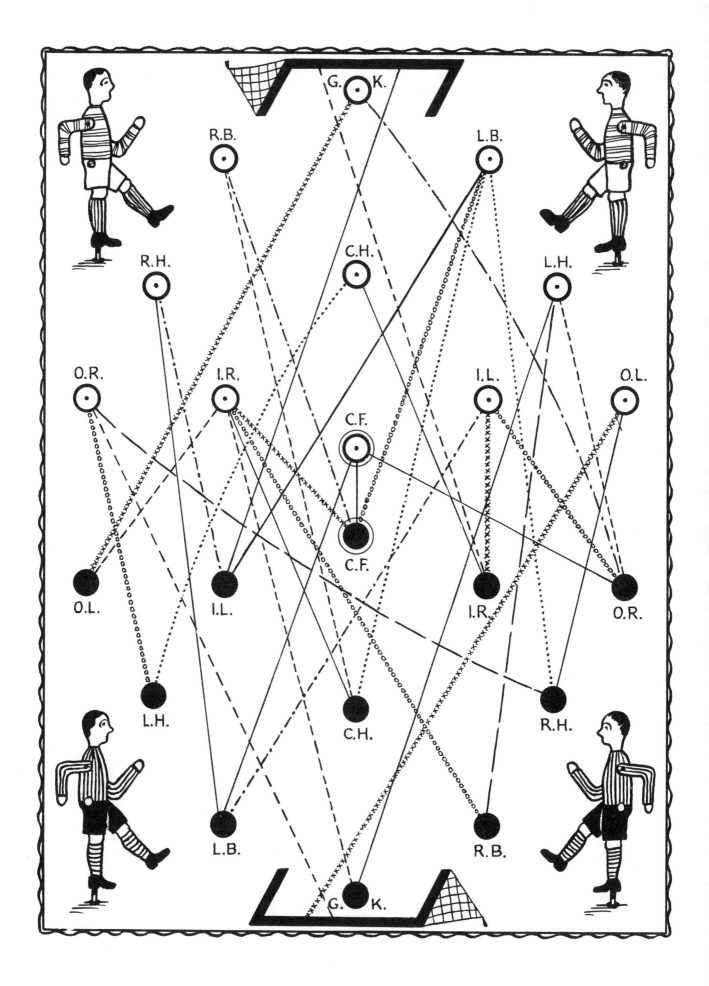

No. 15
A Christmas Tree

Start at the arrow (bottom, left) and collect as many presents as you can from the Christmas tree without retracing your path. You may not use the same paths or junctions twice, and you must finish at the circle (bottom, right).

Note: *It is possible to collect all the presents except two. Which are they?*

No. 16
A Proverb in Practice

"A bird in the hand is worth two in the bush," runs the proverb, and few would doubt it. First find your two birds in the bush, and then start at the arrow (above the finger) and capture one of them by climbing up the branches.

Note: *You may not cross any printed line.*

No. 17
Percy's Problem

Before going camping for the first time with a girlfriend, Percy worried his Aunt Sophonisba for some advice, but all she would say was, "Don't cross your bridges until you come to them!"

On his way back to camp after a lone walk one day, he came to a group of five bridges which put him in mind of his aunt's advice. "Let me see," he said, "I'm sure she told me always to cross bridges when I come to them, and now I have come to five. What shall I do?"

He saw that he could cross all five bridges and still end up in camp, but he had to decide in what order to take them. How many ways are there in which at least two of the bridges are crossed in different order?

Note: *It is possible to calculate the answer mathematically, but it is simpler to letter or number the bridges and write down all the routes you can find.*

No. 18
Unlucky May

The hawthorn or May blossom was considered unlucky for weddings by the Romans, and it is still said to be an unlucky flower to bring into the house. Starting at the arrow (center), take the spray of May blossom out of the house and throw it into the ashcan (bottom, left). You may not use the same path twice, nor cross your tracks, but you drop the 15 petals on the way. In what order must you drop them?

Note: *The real reason why May blossom is unwelcome in the house is that it is fertilized by small flies and emits a rank smell to attract them.*

No. 19
Underground Movement

Start at the arrow (top) and make your way to the headquarters of the Underground Movement. The letters along the correct route spell a four-letter password, but to choose the wrong word will put you on the spot. What is the correct password?

Note: *This is a "solid" maze, as explained in the note to No. 11.*

No. 20
New Year's Eve

Old Father Time winds up the clock for another year, but he has to get to the clock from the cupboard-under-the-stairs without being seen by more than three faces. On his return he wishes "A happy New Year!" to everybody, passing all the faces once, and once only. How does he manage this without traversing the same passage twice on the same journey?

Note: *The first of these two puzzles is easy, but you may find the second quite difficult.*

No. 21
Hit the Coconut

You can visit the "coconut toss" with a friend and see who can score the most with three balls. There is a ball all ready to throw at the starting point.

Note: *Once started, you may not retrace your path but must follow it to the end. If you find yourself back at the start, you may reckon you have missed altogether!*

No. 22
Home on Leave

A lucky G.I. arrives home for Christmas, but he has to get from the depot (top, left) to his home (bottom, right) before the Christmas pudding gets cold! He may not use the same paths twice, nor pass any of his friends' houses (or they are sure to ask him in). How must he go?

When his leave is over he makes his way back to the depot, but this time he calls at all his friends' houses to say goodbye. Once more, he manages this without using the same paths twice, but can you find his route?

Note: *A bit cynical, perhaps, to say "goodbye" to people you've deliberately dodged saying "hello" to, but that's how it goes, folks!*

No. 23
The Magic Barometer

How many different ways are there of getting from STORMY to FINE on this barometer? You may use some of the same paths more than once, for a route counts as "different" so long as a part of it differs from the others. You may also cross your own track at the junctions whenever you like, but you are advised to study the whole diagram carefully and so discover a systematic way of solving the problem.

Note: *A clue is provided in part of the ornamental scrollwork surrounding the barometer. You should be able to spot it if you are thinking along the right lines.*

No. 24
Willie the Worm

Willie the Worm has escaped from the hook, and the fish (top, left) manages to grab him without crossing a line—any sort of line. See if you can find the fish's path first time, but woe betide you for a poor fish if you catch the other worm!

Note: *All legitimate paths and gaps are clear.*

No. 25
Roll Out the Barrel!

Sapper B. Entwhistle was no sap. During some "mopping-up" operations in Italy during World War II, he came across some abandoned wine cellars of enormous extent. There were 70 cellars altogether, and of their 123 doors, 53 were locked. Most of the cellars seemed to be empty, but Sapper Entwhistle had been told by a local farmer that one of them still contained several bottles of wine and a barrel of Chianti, and these he determined to find. Taking some friends with him, he eventually reached the barrel without forcing any of the doors, but since no less than 70 of the doors were open, it is not perhaps surprising that some of the party got lost on the return journey. Which way did Sapper Entwhistle go?

Note: *His lost friends were subsequently traced by means of a trail of broken bottles, but—to tell the absolute truth—that's neither here nor there.*

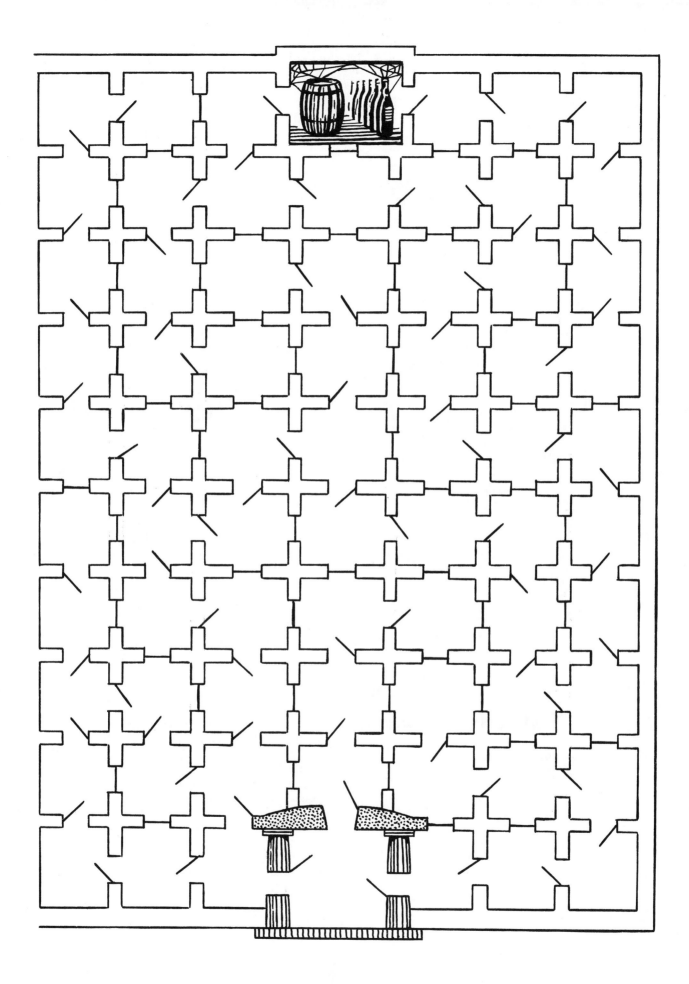

No. 26
Talking Turkey

You may buy a turkey from the butcher, the farmer and the poultry thief. Starting from each in turn, find your way to the turkey, but on your way from the thief you must avoid the London policeman or forfeit your bird. If the price corresponds with the distance you go, which is the cheapest turkey?

Note: *On your three journeys you may use some of the same paths over again, but not on any single journey. (As if you would!) Try to find the shortest path each way.*

No. 27
'Twixt Cup and Lip

Yes—there's many a slip 'twixt cup and lip, as the old proverb says, and this time you pay for your slips in cents or pence or dollars—or whatever you have a yen for (if that means anything!). Starting at the tankard (bottom, left), see if you can convey your beer to the mouth (top, right) without incurring any fines for spilling it on your clothes. Failing a free drink, what is the cheapest you can manage?

Note: *The little arrows indicate spills and the numbers the amounts of the fines.*

No. 28
A Spy Hunt

This is a game for two. Get a friend to pose as the spy (center) and you take the jeep (bottom, right). Making the first move, you then chase the spy from hideout to hideout, moving in turns one stage at a time. Curious, but once you have visited one particular hideout, the spy's capture is absolutely certain, no matter how he dodges. What is that particular hiding place, and what is the least number of moves you need to make in order to catch him?

Note: *It is convenient to use two small counters or buttons for making the moves, and each player must take his turn, even if he merely goes back again to his last hideout.*

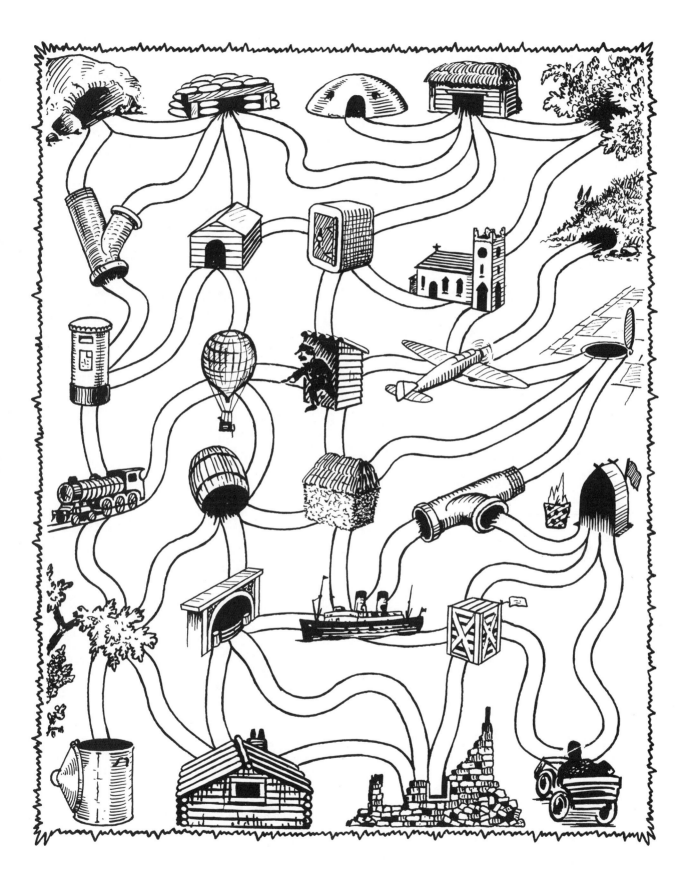

No. 29
Waste Not, Want Not!

Why waste electricity—even if it costs nothing (which it never does)? Starting at the bottom left-hand corner, make your way to the door (top, right), switching off all seven electric lights on the way.

Note: *You may not pass over the same paths twice.*

No. 30
The Chunnel

The Channel Tunnel, dubbed the "Chunnel" by *Punch* and intended to link England with France, was actually begun in 1881. A glance at the diagram opposite shows why it was never finished—the engineers lost their way. See if you can find the shortest way through from Dover to Calais.

Note: *This is a "solid" maze, as explained in the note to No. 11.*

No. 31
Postman's Knock

Starting each time at the bird's-eye view of a man (in the center), choose a "victim" and make your way to his or her cupboard for a kiss. All four "victims" can be reached without using any of the paths twice.

Note: *In the old party game you are called the "postman," and you have no idea who is hiding in the cupboards or empty rooms throughout the house. So you choose a door, knock once, and ask any general question (through the shut door). The person hiding on the other side answers in a disguised voice, and you have to guess whether it belongs to your chosen "victim" or not. If you think not, you pass on to try another door, but if you think you have struck lucky you give the door a double knock (the traditional "postman's knock") and the person inside is then obliged to open up and you must kiss— no matter who it turns out to be. The "victim" then becomes the "postman" for the next round, and the game continues until there is nobody left to kiss.*

No. 32
Here's Luck!

Start with the hikers, at the top, and make your way to the "Horseshoe" in the center for a drink. What are (a) the fewest, and (b) the greatest, number of signposts you can pass on the way without visiting the same signposts twice on the same journey? Remember to include the first signpost in your answer.

Note: *You are required to count the posts—not their direction arms.*

No. 33
The Giant Firecracker

Well, it starts off in the direction of the arrow and, without touching any of the boys, passes through every square once only until the final explosion at the top of the page. Suppose it always moves parallel with the sides of the squares, so that at every change of direction it turns through a right angle. What routes must it take to make exactly 17, 19 and 23 right angles before exploding?

Note: *Count every change from horizontal to vertical, or vice versa, as a right angle, but the lines you draw may actually wave about a bit to avoid touching the boys.*

No. 34
Coil and Recoil

Flap-ear the sailor stared at the complicated coil of heavy ropes before him. There were five frayed ends on the circumference, but of the five ends in the center four were bound and one bore a knot. He had been told to splice a "crown" on the outer end of the knotted cable, but did not know which of the frayed ends belonged to it. The ropes were too heavy to move, so he was busy tracing out the coils by means of a roving eye and a waving marlinespike. Perhaps you could help to disentangle the right rope for him?

Note: *It is quite easy working from the outside inwards to decide which are the four unwanted ends, but the puzzle is to connect up the fifth with the knot in the center.*

No. 35
Welcome Home!

This is another game for two to play, say "dark man" (bottom, left) and "fair man" (bottom, right). Toss for start and take one step at a time in turns. You may move to any unoccupied step, no matter which way the foot is pointing, provided you do not leap over one or cross the continuous black lines. A player may not miss a turn, or return to either of his last two positions, but if he finds himself unable to move because the next step is occupied by his opponent, he must take one step back, counting it as his move.

Now, see who can enter the house in the smallest exact multiple of 7 steps (7, 14, 21, 28, etc.)! Also, guess the total number of footprints illustrated, without counting them.

Note: *The first three steps for both players are numbered.*

No. 36
The Village Postman

In this old English village there are five mailboxes of the "pillar-box" type. Starting at the bottom, the postman visits the four other boxes and finishes at the post office (at the top). If he is not allowed to walk along the same street twice, in how many different ways can he make his collection?

Note: *He is allowed to cross a street he has used before, but not to walk along it (or a part of it).*

No. 37
A Shunting Problem

Bang Clank, the chief shunter at the Clonkrattle Freight Depot, was required to shunt the train on the left, leaving one freight car in each of 16 sidings and finishing in the engine shed on the right. He was allowed to drop cars off either end of the train, but was not allowed to reverse his direction except to come out of a siding. (That is, he could reverse his direction only at the lettered points.) He could, however, use the same tracks as many times as he found necessary so long as he did not visit the same siding twice. In what order did he visit the 16 sidings?

Note: *Use the letters on the sidings to indicate the order.*

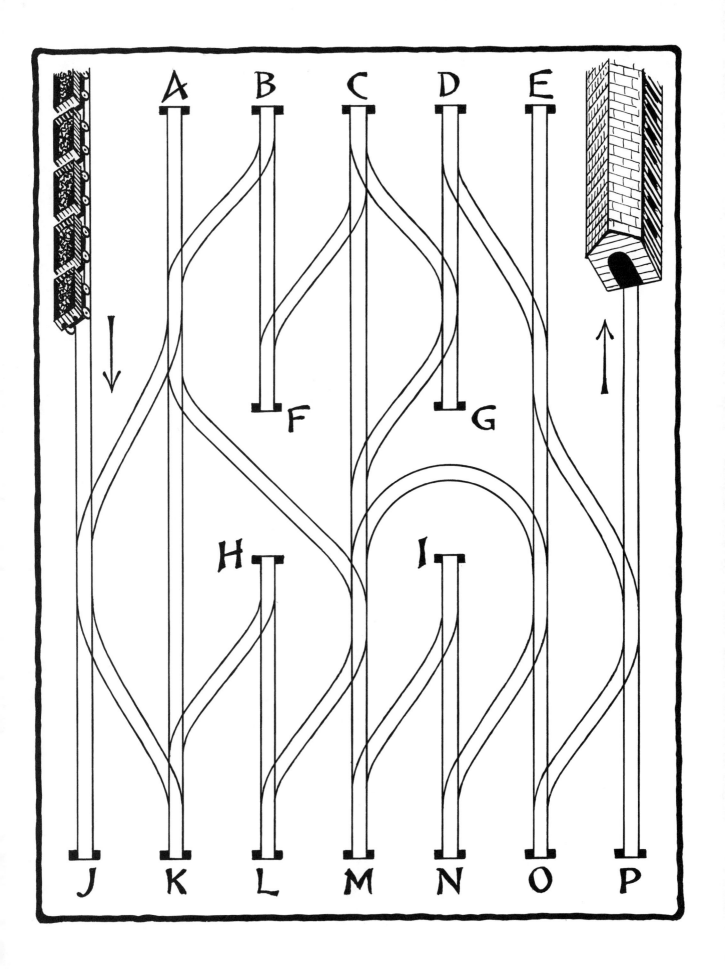

No. 38
Going Camping

In walking from the top of the page
To camp at the foot, you must engage
To break your journey and assuage

Your thirst at these four country inns—
The Ram, Bull, Crab and Heavenly Twins;
The arrow shows where the puzzle begins.

You may visit the inns—'tis all the same—
In any order you care to name,
But you must obey the rules of the game:

Three bridges must be crossed before
Each inn is visited, and three more
Before you enter your canvas door.

However, you may, if you should choose,
When asked to enter an inn, refuse.
(Just passing isn't a visit to booze.)

But watch your step and do not slack,
For as you wander forth and back
You must not cross your own old track.

Note: *The 15 bridges must be crossed only once each.*

No. 39
The Old Nichol

This is a map of the "Old Nichol" in East London (see page ix) as it is today, together with a few extra streets to the north and east. You have received some freight at the Bishopsgate Goods Depot, at the foot of the map. Leaving from either No. 1 or No. 2 exit, make your way to Columbia Market, at the point marked by an X, but you must observe the following curious rule:

Whenever you come to a turning, whether it is to the left or the right of the road you are in, *you must take it*. If there are two turnings, as at a crossroads, you may choose either, and if there are several turnings meeting at a point, you may take any except the continuation of the road you are in. If you run into a blind alley or off the edge of the map, you may do an about-face and return to its entrance. How many turnings do you find you need to take altogether (counting an about-face as two)?

Note: *For a road on the other side of a junction to count as a continuation of the road you are in, it must be exactly opposite. ("Nearly" is not "really"!) To avoid a tiresome headache, be very strict about this.*

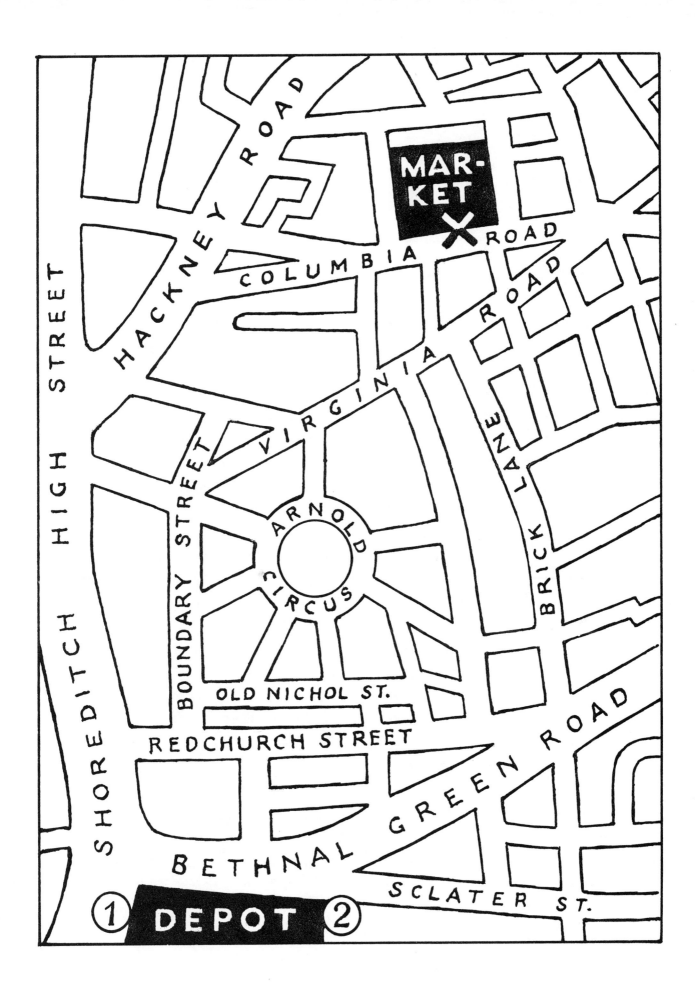

No. 40
Fire! Fire!

Here are three entangled fire hoses. Can you tell the fireman which of the three ends at the bottom belongs to the nozzle he is holding? No "pointers" are allowed—you must trace out the hose *by eye alone.*

Note: *This is a "solid" maze, as explained in the note to No. 11.*

No. 41
The March Hare

There are 31 days in March, and the problem is to "jug" this March hare in exactly 31 moves, counting A, B or C as your first move. You may move only along the lines, and may not visit the same circle twice. The letters along the correct route spell out an appropriate phrase.

Note: *The style of the drawings should give you a hint!*

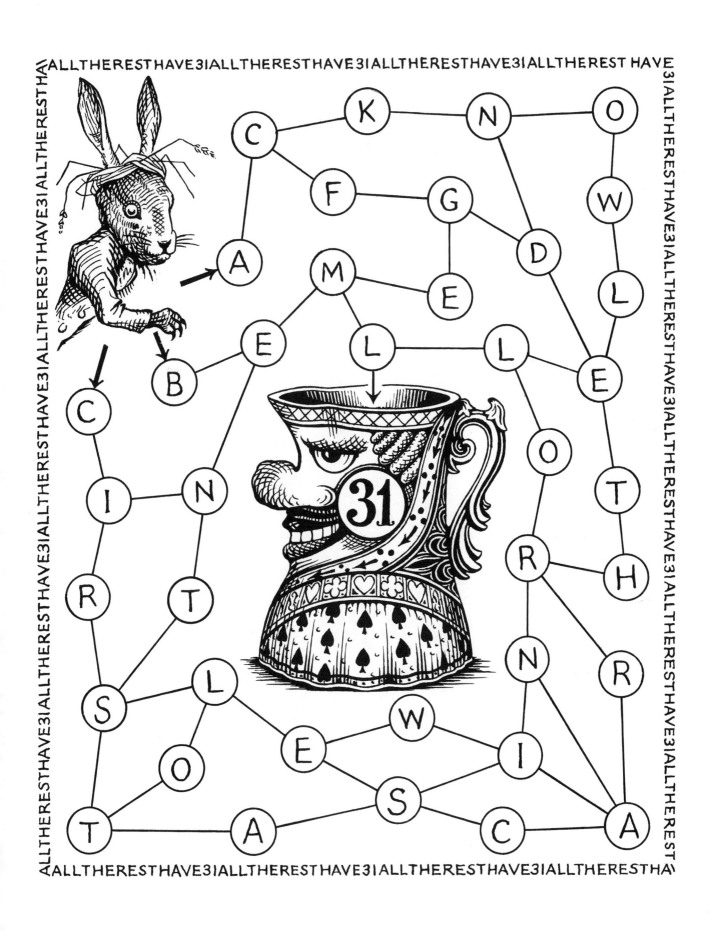

No. 42
A Christmas Cracker

Two people pull this cracker. Which of them will get the prize in the center? Having tossed for first move, each player puts a finger on one of the bells at the ends of the cracker. They then take turns, moving from lantern to lantern along the paper chains. You must stop at each lantern you come to, but may not move to the lantern occupied by your opponent. You may move backwards if you wish (or have to!).

Note: *Each player must take his turn and vacate the lantern he is standing on. No "passing"!*

No. 43
Adjusting the Time

An Englishman, an Irishman and a Scotsman arrived in Chicago from New York and found they had to put their clocks and watches back one hour. The Englishman adjusted his at 10 o'clock, moving the hands from X to IX, but the Irishman waited an hour and moved his from XI to X, while the Scotsman forgot to do it till midnight, when he made the adjustment from XII to XI. Each managed his task without passing through any of the other numbers on the way. How did they do it?

Note: *The three puzzles are separate, so that the same paths may be used more than once.*

WALTER SHEPHERD

No. 44
Getting Away With It

Slippery Sam has just escaped from Swing-Swing Prison by a rope of knotted sheets. A getaway car awaits him on the other side of a wide and dangerous swamp. This is crisscrossed with safe paths, but guards have been stationed at all the strategic points, and Sam's task is to get to the car without passing any of them. Find at least two ways *having no paths in common* by which he may succeed, and also make a guess at the number of guards (large round dots) without counting them.

Note: *You may take ten marks if you never pause or have to retrace your path, but knock one off every time you stop or turn back to try another way.*

No. 45
The Four Winds

The Four Winds, known at about 100 B.C. as Boreas, Notus, Eurus and Zephyrus, blow from the north, south, east and west, respectively—if not respectfully. The sailboat opposite received a buffet from all four of them, and the puzzle is to trace a separate path for each of the winds, starting at the "puffs" (in the corners) and finishing at the pennant (flag) on the masthead of the vessel. The paths may not cross and all legitimate ways are perfectly clear.

Note: *True, the mainsail and jib appear quite steady, but the pennant is certainly "boxing the compass"!*

No. 46
The Surplus Domino

Here is a complete set of dominoes. Starting with the double-blank (in the center), join them end to end in the usual way (5 to 5, 3 to 3, etc.) so as to end with the double-six (bottom, right). This can be done only if one domino is left out. Which is it?

Note: *The answer can be found mathematically, but the easiest way is to do the puzzle first of all on a table with real dominoes.*

No. 47
Put Your Foot in It!

In 1588 many of the ships of the Spanish Armada were wrecked on the coasts of Scotland and Ireland. Most of them carried treasure which the survivors hid in caves or buried, after making rough charts of their positions. Not long ago, one of these charts was found by a Scotsman in a ruined monastery, but being unable to read the Spanish inscription he got a friend, who happened to be an admiral in the Spanish Navy, to translate it for him. It indicated a spot not ten miles distant, so they set out at once to find it.

The Scot, whose name was Darag Frisealach Cruachan Urquhart Mac-a-Bhreatnaich Dalgarno Forbeses of Glenvarloch, Laird of the Isles of Cluny, Eoghan and Auchtermuchty, knew the coast well and objected that a seaside town now occupied the area covered by the chart. However, the Spaniard, who was Almirante Don Pedro Rodriquez Mariano de Miguel y Bruguera de las Asturias Borhorques y Saavedra de Torneros y Beramendi, said that the spot where the treasure had been buried nearly 400 years ago was now a short distance offshore, so they could hire a boat and paddle for it.

This they did, and almost immediately Darag put his toe straight into a chest filled with jewels. The admiral recognized it at once as belonging to his family, but during the violent quarrel which followed the chest fell back into the water. The two bodies were later washed ashore so far from the treasure site that nobody ever guessed what had happened, but if you are careful you can trace the path traversed by Darag's big toe as it found its way down to the jewels.

Note: *It is not permitted to cross a line.*

No. 48
Your Shot!

See how many you can score with three shots on this pinball game! If you run into a "pip" your ball must be considered to drop down a hole and to come up again at any other "pip" of the same suit. Then you continue playing until you score, even if you keep coming back to the starting point. Thus, you should have three scores to add together, but they must be made in different circles. If you land a second time in the same circle it reckons as a complete miss and you have wasted one of your three turns.

Note: *You can arrange a game to play with your friends on this pinball diagram.*

No. 49
Jumping the Queue

In a hundred years' time, when fashions have run full circle back to those shown here, the population of the country will be so great that you will have to queue for everything. Which queue will you join—that for fish, cigarettes, oranges or the cinema? Having got in your queue (in the center), start to elbow your way through to the front so that you can make your purchase. You must follow the lines of the queues, not the spaces between them, and every so often you may have to thread your way through little groups of people. This may confuse you and you could find yourself sidetracked into the wrong queue!

Note: *The cigarettes of the future will doubtless be tobacco-free, so you needn't hesitate to have a smoke.*

No. 50
Man on Mars

The atom bomb conspirator makes a mistake (bottom) and wakes up in Mars (top, left). How does he go—without crossing a line?

Note: *As his comrades wrote in his obituary:*

Nye Hillist tried to make a bomb,
  Nor guessed when he began it
That it would plant him in a tomb
  Upon another planet!

Mad schemes were always being gen-
  erated in his cranium;
His last was to release the en-
  ergy of pure uranium.

Alas! thank goodness he achieved
  The goal of his endeavor,
And now we all may feel relieved
  That he has gone forever!

HOW TO SOLVE A MAZE

The title of this section should really be amended to "How to Try to Solve a Maze," for there is no guaranteed method of solving even the common types of maze. The subject is rather like that of code breaking. To break a code, you must first decide what kind of code it is, and then apply the appropriate technique, and maze puzzles demand a similar approach.

First of all, we may make the fundamental distinction between mazes drawn on paper, in which the whole plan may be seen at once, and "real life" mazes which you can thread only by walking into their passages, where you can never see farther than the next corner. Systems have been devised for solving the simplest examples of both kinds.

A maze which can be seen in plan presents no problems if it contains only a single forced path, but if it offers choices of way to the solver, the *wrong* choices must belong to one of two kinds. In the first, they simply lead into a blind alley from which you can escape only by retracing your path. In the second, they are merely elaborate and pointless perambulations which eventually bring you back to the true path, usually not very far from the point at which you left it. Such digressions do not prevent your reaching your goal, they merely delay it, so that a maze of this kind can hardly be said to be satisfactorily solved until you have found the *shortest* path.

One way to discover the shortest path is first of all to examine the plan in sections to discover its structure, instead of starting off at once to explore the individual paths. The useless perambulations can generally be spotted because they are almost completely enclosed by an unbroken succession of lines. The whole area within such lines may then be eliminated from the puzzle by shading them in with pencil. See Fig. 9, where *x* marks the entrances to two obvious perambulations.

When all the perambulations have been isolated, it remains only to mark off the blind alleys. These are easily recognized, the two in Fig. 9 being labeled *y*. It is necessary only to trace the paths back from these points until a choice of ways is reached, shading over the paths as you go. When all the blind alleys have also been shaded over, only the true shortest path to the center of the maze will be left unshaded.

A real, life-size maze is not open to this sort of treatment. Imagine you have just been put bodily into the center of a real maze, whose high walls or hedges prevent you from seeing more than a few yards in any direction. You might well think that escape can only be a matter of chance, and it would certainly avail you little simply to wander about trying to remember the various directions you were taking.

Yet it is quite easy to escape from such a maze provided all its walls are connected in some way, so that it contains no "islands." All you have to do is to hug the right-hand (*or* the left-hand) wall of the chamber or passage you happen to be in, and to stick to it regardless of any other consideration. Fig. 10A shows clearly why this system must always work in a maze of the kind described.

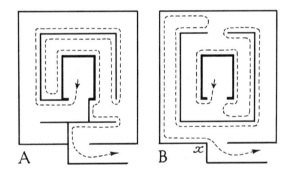

Fig. 10. Finding the way out of a maze whose plan is unknown. A, a maze containing no "islands." B, a maze containing two concentric "islands." In applying Trémaux's rules in B, the escaper could have gone out at the point x on first passing it, but he would have had no knowledge of this and might well have followed the route shown. It is clear that the rules would have enabled him to escape no matter which path he chose.

However, the case is different in a maze containing "islands," like that in Fig. 10B, for if you happen to be on one of the islands and apply the rule just given, you will simply go round and round the island for ever! This snag may be overcome by applying "Trémaux's rules," provided you have with you a piece of chalk or some other means of marking the junctions

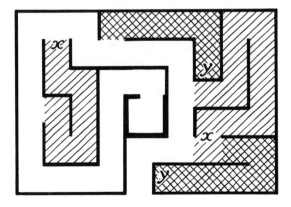

Fig. 9. Finding the shortest path to the center by eliminating perambulations (x) and blind alleys (y).

of the paths as you arrive at them. Trémaux's rules are as follows:

1. No path should be used more than twice.
2. If you arrive at a choice of ways you have never visited before, it does not matter which one you take.
3. When a new path leads you to a junction of ways you have visited before, or into a blind alley, retrace your steps to where you entered it.
4. When an old path leads you to a junction of ways you have visited before, take a new path if possible; if not, take any of the others.

These practical methods of solving mazes become less easy to apply as the mazes increase in complexity, but more oblique methods are then sometimes feasible. For example, if the maze is seen in plan and clearly contains a great many choices of ways, it may be an advantage to redraw it in simplified form. The method to be described is often very helpful in problems which ask for more than just a path to the center. There may be several alternative routes, and the puzzle may not be just to find the shortest (or longest) path, but to find how many different, or partly different, paths there are. Fig. 11 is a maze problem of this sort, and Fig. 12 shows the kind of simplified pattern to which it can be reduced.

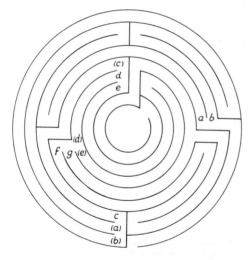

Fig. 11. A typical maze in which the problem is to discover the number of different ways in which it may be threaded.

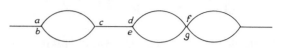

Fig. 12. The simplified pattern to which the maze in Fig. 11 may be reduced by the method described in the text.

The method is to enter the maze and proceed until you come to the first choice of ways. If there are two of these, their entrances are labeled a and b, respectively. Each is then followed until the next choice of ways is reached, where it is closed by repeating its letter in brackets. At the same time, letters are allocated to each of the new paths and these are followed round in the same manner. Each stretch of the maze between one choice of ways and the next can then be represented without its elaborate windings by a short line, as shown in Fig. 12, and from the result it is easy to calculate the answer.

In this example, the maze threader is soon offered a choice of two ways, at a and b. Whichever one he follows, he is obliged to continue along c, but so far the number of possible routes is 2. At the further end of c he is faced with the choice of d and e, and he has this choice whichever of the two previous routes he may have taken, so the total possibility is now 4. But d and e both lead him to a point where he has to choose between g and h, so that each of his four routes may continue from here in two different ways, making a total of 8. There are no more choices, so that 8 is the answer. It is much easier to solve the maze in this way than to try to trace round all the routes separately (say with differently colored pencils—if you have enough!) and then count them up.

It is possible to solve a great many of the less orthodox maze puzzles by similar mathematical means, but since their variety is endless there are no all-embracing principles to be given, nor is the required mathematics always easy. In any case, the characteristic fun of a maze lies in threading it, and only if this is really impracticable would the devout mazer resort to other means.

For he who would escape the artful maze
Must master all its weary, wand'ring ways,
Retracing many steps, and suff'ring long delays,
Until, at last, the open Portal greets his gaze!

SOLUTIONS

No. 1 A Lunch Date

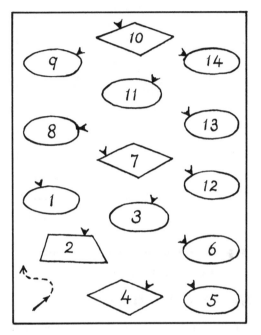

The tables are numbered in the order of visiting, and the arrowheads show where their tops should be touched.

No. 2 A Flight of Fancy

Turn to the right halfway up the left-hand path and after that (at the successive choices of ways) go: left, (left), left, right, right, (right), left. The words in brackets mean that though a choice has to be made, the correct path does, in fact, run straight ahead.

No. 3 The Man in the Moon

It is easy to find all the answers to this one by tracing the paths backwards, and they do not rate an explanatory diagram.

No. 4 A Mayday Frolic

A holds ribbon 2; B holds 3; and C holds 1.

No. 5 Weathercock-a-doodle-Do!

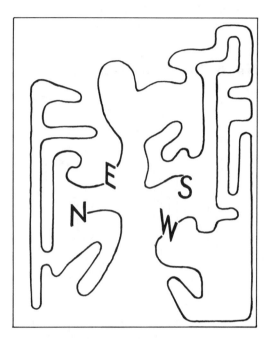

SEWN, WENS, WEN, SEW, NEW, WE, EN (the name of the fourteenth letter of the alphabet; also a typographical unit).

No. 6 Bad Karl's Cavern

In this type of puzzle, each cave or cell can be entered *and* left again only if it has an even number of doors. If it has an odd number of doors, like the one Bad Karl starts from, it can either be permanently vacated or must finally be permanently occupied (supposing that all the doors have to be used). The diagram shows the only caves with an odd number of doors, but the two on the left may be treated as having only two doors each if the one connecting them is ignored. Thus, Karl need leave only this one door unused, passing through all the other 37 in any of several possible orders, without crossing his own path.

No. 8 Guy Fawkes Night

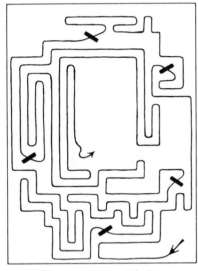

The correct match is D.

No. 9 Collecting Your Baggage

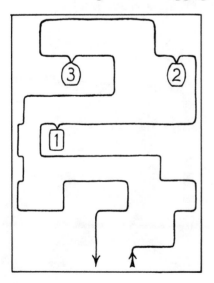

No. 10 Start the Day Clean!

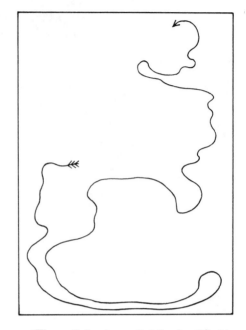

(The path has been slightly simplified.)

No. 11 Ringing the Changes

CDBA,   CDBB,   CDAB,   CDAA

No. 12 Color Bars

You must call at the bars in the following order: Blue Boar, Red Lion, Green Man, White Hart, Red Deer, Dun Cow, Black Horse, Pink Pig.

No. 13 The Four Seasons

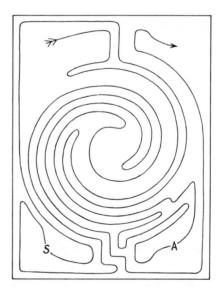

The "silly season" comes traditionally towards the end of summer, when the politicians, lawyers, university professors, and big businessmen are all away on holiday. Since nothing "important" can then happen, the news items and topics of conversation tend to be of a trivial or "silly" nature.

No. 15 A Christmas Tree

The presents must be collected in the following order, starting with either the soap or the model airplane: chocolates, socks, diary, wine, doll, hand mirror, stockings, alarm clock, necklace, bath salts, toy, necktie. The two you cannot collect, if you take the maximum possible, are the railway engine and either the soap or the airplane.

No. 16 A Proverb in Practice

Take the right-hand fork and ascend the tree to the right of the tall black shoot. Then, by zigzagging round the top left part of the tree you can descend and catch the left-hand bird.

No. 17 Percy's Problem

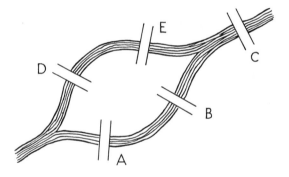

Percy can cross the five bridges in 16 different ways. If we letter the bridges as in the diagram, the possible ways are as follows:

ADEBC	BDEAC	CEBAD	ABCED
ADCBE	BDCAE	CEABD	ABCDE
AEDBC	BEDAC	CDABE	BACED
AECBD	BECAD	CDBAE	BACDE

No. 18 Unlucky May

The petals must be dropped in the following order: K-G-C-E-D-B-F-H-J-L-M-O-N-I-A

No. 19 Underground Movement

The password is PALS.

No. 20 New Year's Eve

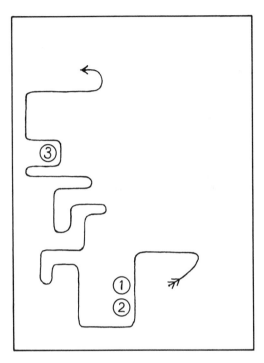

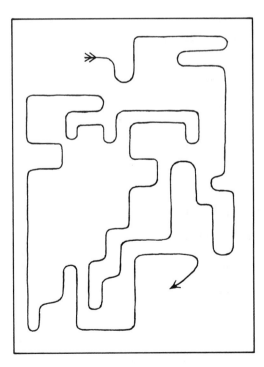

No. 22 Home on Leave

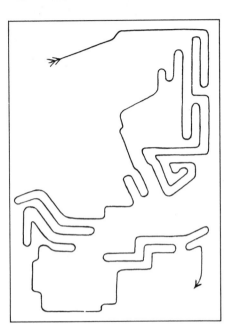

No. 23 The Magic Barometer

There are 9 different (or partly different) ways of getting from STORMY to FINE. The clue is provided by the supporting scroll, which is a curved line carrying two loops. Each of these loops represents a junction of 4 ways, and since you must arrive along one of them you have a choice of 3 to follow. No matter which of the first 3 you choose, you still have a choice of 3 at the second junction, and $3 \times 3 = 9$.

No. 24 Willie the Worm

The fish starts by doubling round its own tail and zigzagging down the left edge of the picture. It then weaves over to the right side, passing a little below the lower worm and almost reaching the fisherman's right knee. Traveling up under the arch of the rod, it finally comes down again beneath the line to catch Willie in the act of escaping.

No. 25 Roll Out the Barrel!

Enter by the left-hand door and turn right, traveling up the diagram in the column to the left of the door. At the fourth row, turn left and then right twice in succession. At the next choice of ways you work right back towards the bottom right-hand corner of the plan. You then proceed up the right-hand side without further difficulty, and finally enter the wine cellar by its left-hand door.

No. 26 Talking Turkey

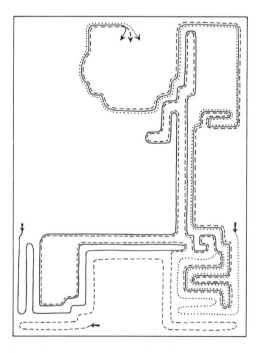

The farmer's turkey is the cheapest.

No. 27 'Twixt Cup and Lip

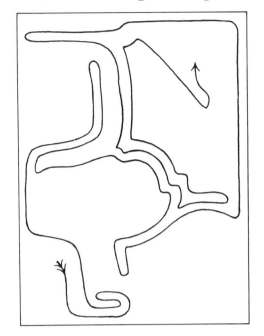

No. 28 A Spy Hunt

The hideout you must visit to make the spy's capture certain is the cave (top left corner), and you can catch him in as few as 17 moves.

No. 29 Waste Not, Want Not!

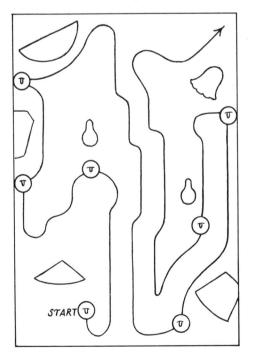

No. 30 The Chunnel

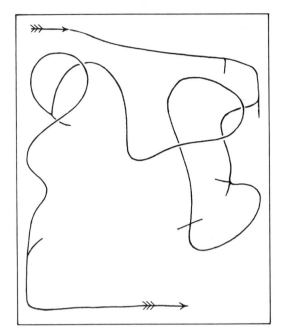

No. 31 Postman's Knock

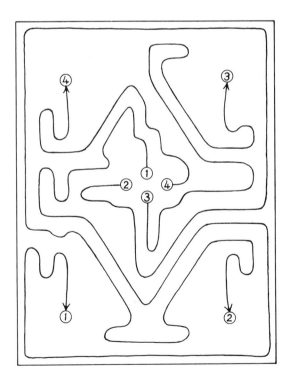

No. 32 Here's Luck!

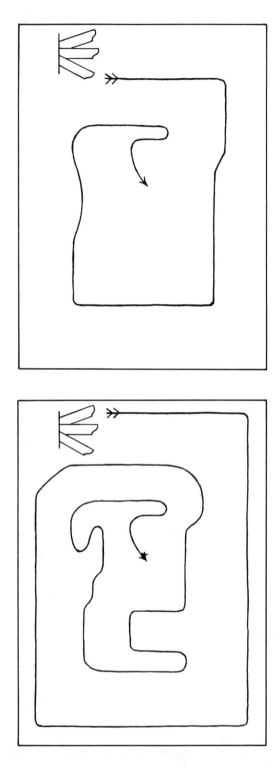

The fewest number of signposts is three, the greatest five.

No. 33 The Giant Firecracker

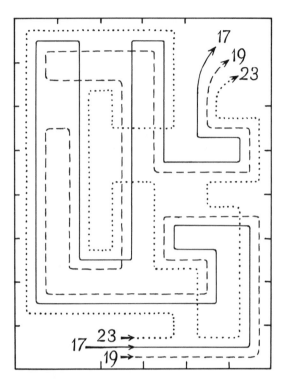

No. 34 Coil and Recoil

The correct outer end is the right-hand one of the bottom pair. The solution, if not seen, can then be found easily by trial and error.

No. 35 Welcome Home!

There are 42 footprints.

No. 36 The Village Postman

He can make his collection in six different ways, visiting the pillar-boxes in any of the following orders:

abdc   cadb   dcab
acdb   cbda   dcba

No. 37 A Shunting Problem

The sidings should be visited in the following order:
J-A-K-H-L-B-F-C-G-D-N-I-M-O-E-P

No. 38 Going Camping

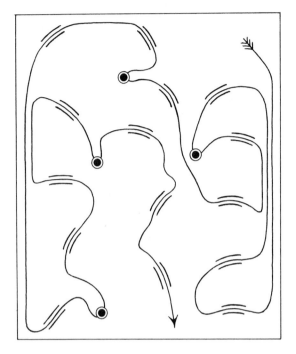

No. 43 Adjusting the Time

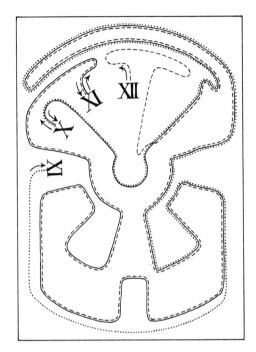

No. 44 Getting Away With It

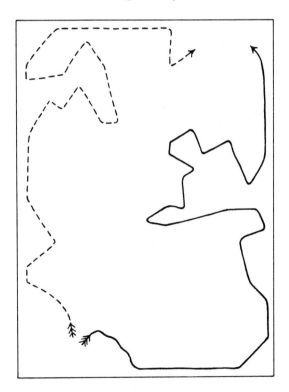

No. 39 The Old Nichol

The best route is to leave at Exit No. 2 and go down Sclater Street. Zigzagging according to the rules, you can then get to Arnold Circus after 8 turns. Leaving the Circus by the horizontal "spoke" on its right side, you next turn to the left, but go right at the "I" in VIRGINIA and left again at the "A"—and so home, having taken 14 turnings altogether.

No. 40 Fire! Fire!

The fireman's nozzle is attached to the left-hand intake end.

No. 41 The March Hare

The phrase spelled out on the correct route is: ACKNOWLEDGEMENTS TO LEWIS CARROLL.

There are 36 guards.

No. 45 The Four Winds

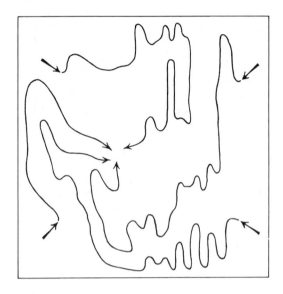

No. 50 Man on Mars

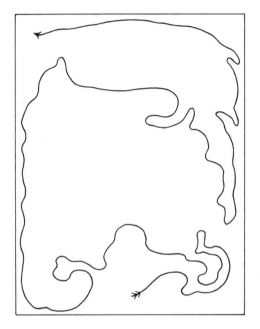

No. 46 The Surplus Domino

Since in a complete set of dominoes each number, from 0 to 6, occurs an even number of times (8, in fact), if you join them all in a row, matching number to number, the odd number at the end must be the same as the number at the beginning. So if you are to begin with 0-0 and end with 6-6, the 0-6 must be left out. There are several ways of arranging the remaining dominoes, for example: 0-0, 0-3, 3-2, 2-4, 4-1, 1-3, 3-3, 3-5, 5-0, 0-2, 2-2, 2-1, 1-1, 1-0, 0-4, 4-4, 4-3, 3-6, 6-4, 4-5, 5-5, 5-6, 6-2, 2-5, 5-1, 1-6, 6-6.

No. 47 Put Your Foot in It!

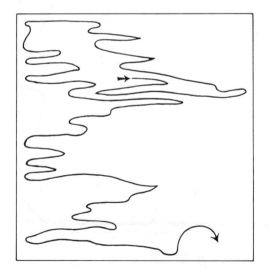